Artists Around the World

Meet some of the greatest artists of all time

ENCYCLOPÆDIA

Britannica®

CHICAGO   LONDON   NEW DELHI   PARIS   SEOUL   SYDNEY   TAIPEI   TOKYO

© 2004 BY ENCYCLOPÆDIA BRITANNICA, INC.

Cover photos (front): Archivo Iconografico, S.A./Corbis; (back): Julie Lemberger/Corbis. Cover insert photos (left): Bettmann/Corbis; (centre): Robbie Jack/Corbis; (right): Hulton-Deutsch Collection/Corbis.

International Standard Book Number: 1-59339-036-X

No part of this work may be reproduced or utilized in any form or by any means, electronic or mechanical, including photocopying, recording, or by any information storage and retrieval system, without permission in writing from the publisher.

BRITANNICA LEARNING LIBRARY: ARTISTS AROUND THE WORLD 2004

Britannica.com may be accessed on the Internet at http://www.britannica.com.

(Trademark Reg. U.S. Pat. Off.) Printed in Singapore.

Artists Around the World

INTRODUCTION

How did Michelangelo paint the ceiling of the Sistine Chapel? Who was Basho?
Where was Kiri Te Kanawa born? What is 'scat' singing?

In *Artists Around the World,* you'll discover answers to these questions and many more. Through pictures, articles, and fun facts, you'll learn about the many kinds of art and meet some of the greatest artists of yesterday and today.

To help you on your journey, we've provided the following signposts in *Artists Around the World*:

■ **Subject Tabs**—The coloured box in the upper corner of each right-hand page will quickly tell you the article subject.

■ **Search Lights**—Try these mini-quizzes before and after you read the article and see how much - *and how quickly* - you can learn. You can even make this a game with a reading partner. (Answers are upside down at the bottom of one of the pages.)

■ **Did You Know?**—Check out these fun facts about the article subject. With these surprising 'factoids', you can entertain your friends, impress your teachers, and amaze your parents.

■ **Picture Captions**—Read the captions that go with the photos. They provide useful information about the article subject.

■ **Vocabulary**—New or difficult words are in **bold type**. You'll find them explained in the Glossary at the end of the book.

■ **Learn More!**—Follow these pointers to related articles in the book. These articles are listed in the Table of Contents and appear on the Subject Tabs.

Britannica®

LEARNING LIBRARY

Have a great trip!

Van Gogh's paintings of sunflowers are probably some of the most famous paintings in the world. You may even have seen them on T-shirts and coffee mugs. This is a photo of an original, painted in 1889.

Artists Around the World
TABLE OF CONTENTS

Lonely Landscapes

Xia Gui is known today as one of China's greatest masters of **landscape** painting. He painted rapidly, using short, sharp strokes of the brush. Most of his landscapes were done in shades of black, but a few had light washes of colour added to them.

Xia was probably the official court painter to either the emperor Ningzong or the emperor Lizong (or maybe both). That means he would have lived about the end of the 12th century to the beginning of the 13th century.

Together with his friend and fellow artist Ma Yuan, Xia founded the Ma-Xia school of painting. This group followed a tradition of very simple landscape painting, with little happening in the landscape and few details. By showing only selected features, such as mountain peaks and twisted trees, they aimed to create a feeling of unlimited space and quiet drama. The Ma-Xia school had a great influence on later artists.

Most of Xia's surviving works are album leaves. These were single sheets of usually square paper, occasionally glued onto fans. The paintings were done on silk, mainly in shades of black ink. In each landscape there are distant hills in the upper left corner and a closer view of land in the lower right corner. In the centre, groups of trees reach into the empty space all around. The empty space was always an important feature of Xia's work.

Xia was also a master at **composing** works on the hand scroll. These are viewed by unrolling the scroll from one end to the other, then rerolling the scroll as you view it. The effect is like a continuous imaginary journey through the scenery of nature.

LEARN MORE! READ THESE ARTICLES…
BASHO · MICHELANGELO · VINCENT VAN GOGH

SEARCH LIGHT

Fill in the gaps: Xia Gui made his paintings on album leaves and

_____ _____.

The painting here, known as 'Swinging Gibbon', is said to be by Xia Gui. The next generation of painters did not value Xia's work. But about 50 years after that, one critic wrote: 'His works have an exciting [stimulating] quality,…a remarkable achievement.'

GALWAY COUNTY LIBRARIES

Answer: Xia Gui made his paintings on album leaves and hand scrolls.

The Sadat Resthouse (built in Garf Huseyn, Egypt, in 1981) shows some of Hassan Fathy's trademark features. Here you can see the thick walls and air scoops that help cool the building naturally.

8

Home-style Architect

Hassan Fathy is famous as a **humanitarian** architect. He built homes and buildings that put people's needs first. Fathy was born in 1900 in Alexandria, Egypt. He studied there and began his career in Egypt.

Fathy's goal was to build **affordable** housing for local Egyptian people. He felt that many European building methods and designs that had come into his country were not well suited to it. He thought houses should be built from local materials, according to local designs, and with traditional methods. By building in this way he lowered the cost of his houses and respected the culture of the area as well. In addition, traditional methods and materials tended to suit the local climate best.

Because Egypt is a very hot country, it is important to plan houses that are as cool as possible. Fathy's buildings often had thick walls (to keep out the heat) surrounding an interior courtyard. Air scoops on the roof caught

The New Gourna Village was built from
a) sticks.
b) straw.
c) mud.

Hassan Fathy.
Courtesy of the Aga Khan Trust for Culture

winds from the desert and funnelled them down through the buildings. By these methods, Fathy managed to cool his buildings naturally.

One of Fathy's most famous creations was the New Gourna Village near Luxor, Egypt. The original village was near the **archaeological** digs of ancient Luxor and had to be relocated. Fathy trained the local people in the ancient tradition of mud brick construction. The people then built homes for themselves that were made almost entirely from mud bricks and that kept all the good features of their former homes.

Fathy died in 1989, but his work has inspired many young architects in the Middle East. He promoted ideas that adapted traditional styles and methods to the needs of the present day.

LEARN MORE! READ THESE ARTICLES…
CHARLES DICKENS • NUSRAT FATEH ALI KHAN • MICHELANGELO

Answer: c) mud.

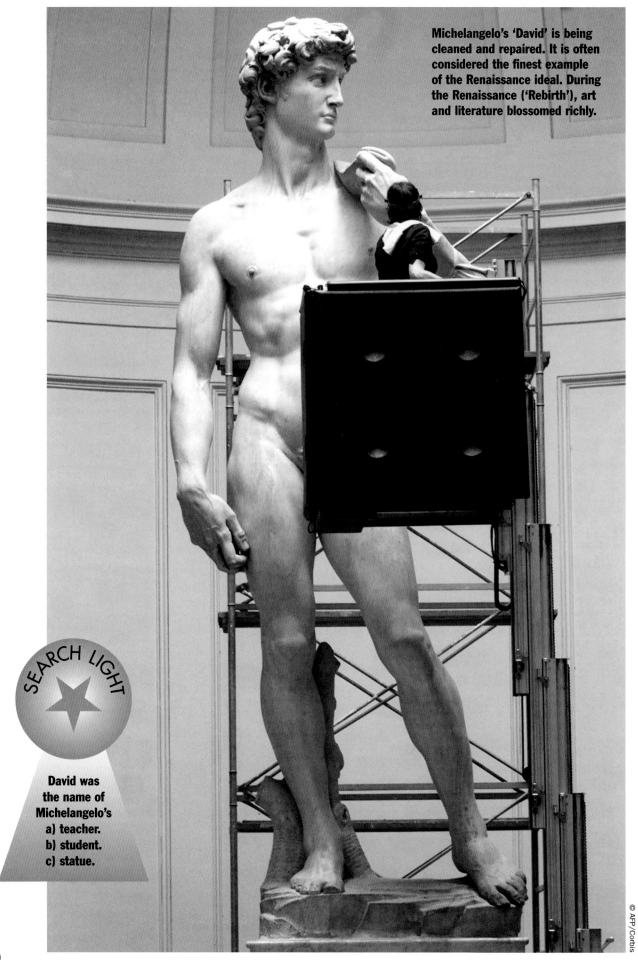

Michelangelo's 'David' is being cleaned and repaired. It is often considered the finest example of the Renaissance ideal. During the Renaissance ('Rebirth'), art and literature blossomed richly.

SEARCH LIGHT

David was the name of Michelangelo's
a) teacher.
b) student.
c) statue.

Genius of European Art

Once there was a small boy in Florence who loved to watch painters and sculptors at work. He wanted to be an artist, but his father did not like the idea. Little did the man know that his son Michelangelo would become one of the world's most famous artists.

Michelangelo began training as an artist at age 13. He was so interested in his art that he often forgot to eat and slept on the floor beside his unfinished artwork. He refused help, even on big projects, so some works took years to complete. Many were never finished.

Michelangelo worked in Rome and Florence. In Rome he was **commissioned** to carve a Pietà. This is a marble statue showing the Virgin Mary supporting the dead Christ on her knees. The finished work, known as the 'Madonna della Pietà', made him famous. And in Florence, Michelangelo spent two years working on a huge block of marble. From it he carved 'David', one of the world's finest and best-known sculptures.

(Top) Portrait of Michelangelo. (Bottom) Michelangelo's frescoes on the Sistine Chapel ceiling and west wall (behind the altar).

Between 1508 and 1512 Michelangelo created his most famous work, the paintings on the ceiling of the Sistine Chapel in the Vatican in Rome. He painted much of the ceiling lying on his back in a tight cramped position. The **fresco** paintings of figures and events from the Bible are huge and splendid. The wall behind the altar **depicts** the Last Judgment of humanity by God.

Michelangelo was so admired that he became the first European artist whose life story was written during his own lifetime.

LEARN MORE! READ THESE ARTICLES...
LUDWIG VAN BEETHOVEN • FRANCISCO DE GOYA • XIA GUI

DID YOU KNOW?
Despite all the time that went into his artwork, Michelangelo found time to design buildings, write poems, and even create defensive structures for Florence.

Frida
Kahlo's
most famous
paintings were
a) murals.
b) self-portraits.
c) buses.

The Brilliant Colours of Mexico

Mexican painter Frida Kahlo's life was filled with struggles. But her dazzlingly colourful **self-portraits** reflect Kahlo's power and confidence in the face of her hardships.

When Kahlo was a child she had polio, and the disease kept her right leg from growing properly. Then, when she was 18, Kahlo was in a terrible bus accident. For the rest of her life she had many operations to try to correct both of these problems.

Kahlo began to paint while she was recovering from the bus accident. Her paintings were often dramatic self-portraits that showed Kahlo's powerful feelings about herself and the world she lived in. Their brilliant colours reflect Kahlo's bold attitude toward life.

Before the bus accident, Kahlo had met the famous Mexican painter Diego Rivera while he was painting a **mural** at her school. Later she showed Rivera some of her paintings and he encouraged her to keep working at her art.

Kahlo and Rivera were married in 1929. They travelled to the United States where Rivera had received **commissions** for murals. Kahlo kept painting and met many important people of the time. The artist Pablo Picasso admired her work. And many of her well-known friends helped her show her paintings in Europe and America.

Kahlo's work was called 'surrealistic' by some. Surrealism is a style of art that has a strange dreamlike quality. Kahlo, however, said that her paintings were the reality that she felt and that they spanned both reality and dreams.

In the spring of 1953 Kahlo had the only exhibition of her work in Mexico. She died one year later. Today her house in Coyoacán is the Frida Kahlo Museum.

LEARN MORE! READ THESE ARTICLES…
SARAH BERNHARDT • FRANCISCO DE GOYA
VINCENT VAN GOGH

DID YOU KNOW?
Kahlo was very proudly Mexican. She often wore very decorative Mexican jewellery and native clothing. Her hairstyle, piled high on her head, was also in the style of the people of the Mexican state of Oaxaca.

Frida Kahlo was the first Hispanic woman to be featured on a U.S. postage stamp. The stamp, seen here being unveiled, featured one of her famous self-portraits.
© AFP/Corbis

Answer: b) self-portraits.

Sunflowers and Starry Nights

SEARCH LIGHT

Vincent van Gogh was a Dutch artist of the 19th century and is now considered to be one of the greatest painters in the world. Van Gogh painted what he saw around him - trees, flowers, people, and buildings. He visited museums and met with other painters. But van Gogh had his own way of painting. He said he 'wanted to look at nature under a brighter sky.'

How many paintings did van Gogh sell in his lifetime?
a) 80
b) 700
c) 1

In van Gogh's paintings, the southern French town of Arles is like no other place in the world. The skies are bluer and the sun is brighter. The orchards in bloom are pinker and greener. The cobblestone streets are more cobbled and stony. His pictures seem to be flooded with a golden light.

Van Gogh wanted wonderful colour in his pictures. His paintings called 'Sunflowers', 'Irises', and 'Starry Night' are among the most famous pictures he painted and are filled with brilliant colours. He tried to keep to the outward appearance of his subjects, yet his feelings about them exploded in strong colour and bold lines.

Self-portrait of van Gogh, painted in 1889.
© Archivo Iconografico, S.A./Corbis

Van Gogh's style was direct, forceful, and natural. He worked with great speed and excitement. He was set on capturing an effect or a mood while it possessed him. He told his brother that if anyone said a painting was done too quickly, 'you can reply that they have looked at it too fast.'

Van Gogh painted for just ten years. But during this time he did more than 800 paintings in oil colours and 700 drawings. Surprisingly, he sold only one painting while he lived. People did not understand the way he painted. His work was too unusual and alive with energy.

Now the whole world knows he was a great artist.

LEARN MORE! READ THESE ARTICLES...
FRIDA KAHLO • PABLO PICASSO • XIA GUI

Van Gogh's paintings of sunflowers are probably some of the most famous paintings in the world. You may even have seen them on T-shirts and coffee mugs. This is a photo of an original, painted in 1889.
© Christie's Images/Corbis

Answer: c) 1

Painter to the King
and to the People

As a young man in Spain, Francisco de Goya worked as a bull-fighter. But his great love was painting. After studying art in Rome, Goya returned to Spain and worked as a **tapestry** designer. Soon his talents attracted attention and he began painting portraits of wealthy Spaniards. By 1786 Goya had become a 'painter to the king of Spain'.

But Goya became tired of painting pictures of dukes and duchesses and the royal family. Most of the people of Spain were poor and often hungry.

Goya's self-portrait at the age of 69.
© Francis G. Mayer/Corbis

Constant wars made their lives worse. Wanting to portray this 'everyday' world, Goya began to draw and paint images of the poor and hardworking people of Spain.

Goya didn't make the men and women in his art look prettier or more important than they were. His paintings show people as they looked after a life of hard work. Goya included the lines in their faces and the sadness in their lives. He showed their bent backs and their worn clothes. This style of painting people and scenes from daily life is called 'realism'.

The subjects of Goya's paintings did not always please the king and the people of the royal court. They thought he should paint only famous people and beautiful things. In fact, his 'Disasters of War' series of etchings was so realistic and **gory** that it was not shown until over 35 years after Goya's death. But today, hundreds of years later, the power and honesty of Goya's 'everyday' paintings still impress and move viewers.

LEARN MORE! READ THESE ARTICLES...
CHARLES DICKENS • PABLO PICASSO • VINCENT VAN GOGH

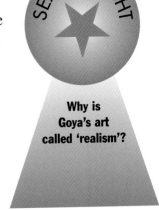

SEARCH LIGHT

Why is Goya's art called 'realism'?

Goya's pictures of everyday life include some pleasant moments such as this one, titled 'Two Boys with Two Mastiffs'. (As you've probably guessed, a mastiff is a large breed of dog.)

© Archivo Iconografico, S.A./Corbis

Answer: Goya's painting style was called 'realism' because he showed ordinary people as they really were.

Exploring
with an Artist

There's a story which says that the artist Pablo Picasso started to draw before he learned to speak. While this is probably only a story, it does suggest how important art was to Picasso.

Picasso was born in Spain in 1881 but lived much of his life in France. He was an inventor and an explorer. But he didn't invent machines or explore strange places. He explored and invented with

Visitors viewing Picasso's painting 'Mandolin, Fruit Bowl, and Plaster Arm'.
© AFP/Corbis

SEARCH LIGHT

What does it mean to say that Picasso's studio was a jungle? (Hint: Jungles are hard to walk through.)

art. He painted with his fingers, made drawings with a rusty nail, and even made a bull's head from the handlebars and seat of a bicycle. He was able to work anywhere at any time of the day or night.

Picasso's big studio was a sort of jungle - a jungle of paint cans, brushes, chalk, pottery, coloured pencils, and crayons, among many other things. Rolls of heavy paper and canvas, picture frames and easels, and tools for cutting designs on heavy board lay scattered about like rubbish. But to Picasso it was all **inspiration**.

He painted Spanish bullfighting, horse races, and clowns. He painted happy pictures in warm colours (such as pink) and sad, lonely ones in cool colours (such as dark blue). He sometimes painted people and animals the way they were. But more often he painted them from his imagination.

The art style that Picasso and fellow artist Georges Braque invented is called Cubism. They painted people and things so that all parts and sides could be seen at the same time. Cubists often created pictures from simple shapes such as squares or cubes.

LEARN MORE! READ THESE ARTICLES…
FRANCISCO DE GOYA • FRIDA KAHLO • XIA GUI

In 2001 the works of Picasso were shown for the first time in China. These children are practising drawing by imitating some Picasso prints. A large photo of the artist looks on from the wall.
© Reuters NewMedia Inc./Corbis

DID YOU KNOW?
Picasso was probably the single most influential figure in 20th-century Western art. And he worked for 80 of his 91 years. He experimented with a large variety of styles in a number of artistic mediums.

Answer: Picasso's studio was so cluttered with art supplies that it was difficult to move around in it. Just as jungles are rich and dense with plant and animal life, so his studio was crowded with materials that helped him create.

Uruguayan President Jorge Batlle (left) and Argentine
Chancellor Adalberto Rodríguez Giavariani admire a
portrait of Jorge Luis Borges painted by Jorge Demirjian.

Creator of Fantastical Fictions

Can you imagine a garden where a beautiful poppy flower has the power to unravel time? Or a pool where if you gaze too long into it, you could merge with your reflection? Jorge Luis Borges imagined these things and more as he created **fantastical** worlds with his words.

Borges was born in 1899, in Buenos Aires, Argentina. His father was a lawyer and his mother was a teacher. His English-born grandmother told him many stories. Borges was educated at home by an English governess and learned English before Spanish.

Borges on his 82nd birthday, in 1981.
© Bettmann/Corbis

At age 20 Borges started writing poems, essays, and a biography. But when his father died in 1938, Borges had to take up a job as a librarian to support the family. The same year, Borges suffered a severe head wound that left him near death, unable to speak, and afraid he was insane. This experience seems to have freed in him a great creativity. When he finished his library work, he would spend the rest of the day reading and writing.

Borges' dreamlike short stories would later make him famous when they were collected in the books *Ficciones* (*Fictions*) and *The Aleph and Other Stories, 1933-69.* He also wrote political articles that angered the Argentine government and cost him his library job.

In 1956 Borges received Argentina's national prize for literature. But he had been losing his eyesight for decades because of a rare disease and by this time he was completely blind. Still, he created stories by having his mother and friends write as he **dictated**. Some of his best work was produced this way, including *El libro de los seres imaginarios* (*The Book of Imaginary Beings*).

LEARN MORE! READ THESE ARTICLES…
ISABEL ALLENDE • LUDWIG VAN BEETHOVEN • JULES VERNE

SEARCH LIGHT

Although Borges is famous as a Spanish-language writer, what language did he learn first?

Answer: Because his governess was English, Borges learned English before Spanish.

21

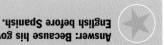

SEARCH LIGHT

Find and correct the mistake in the following sentence: Walker was the first Aboriginal woman to be noticed.

As a young woman, Kath Walker was angry about how Aboriginal people were treated. She then began working to have the laws made more fair - and she succeeded in many ways.

Aboriginal Poet

She was born Kathleen Jean Mary Ruska, but she's known in the Aboriginal language as Oodgeroo Noonuccal. Her Aboriginal last name,

Kath Walker (Aboriginal name Oodgeroo Noonuccal) as an older woman.
National Archives of Australia/Canberra, Act, Australia

Noonuccal, is the name of her clan. Kath Walker, the name she wrote under for most of her career, became a famous Australian Aboriginal writer and political protester. In fact, when her book of poetry, *We Are Going,* came out in 1964, she became the first Aboriginal woman to be published.

Walker grew up in Queensland, Australia, where many of the ancient Aboriginal customs were still practiced. At the time Walker was growing up, Aboriginal people had few rights in Australia. She was allowed to go to school only through the primary grades.

When she was 13, Walker began work as a maid. At 16 she wanted to become a nurse but wasn't allowed to because she was Aboriginal. What Walker did instead was work hard for Aboriginal rights. In 1967 she was successful in getting the anti-Aboriginal sections removed from the Australian constitution. In recognition of her efforts, she was awarded the MBE (Member of the Order of the British Empire) in 1970. Walker would later give back this award to protest further discrimination against Aboriginal people. After 1981 most of her work was published under her Aboriginal name.

Walker described her poetry as easy to understand, with simple rhymes and images. Her work focuses on the troubles of the Aboriginal people. Below is a sample of her poetry.

> But I'll tell instead of brave and fine
> when lives of black and white entwine.
> And men in brotherhood combine,
> this would I tell you, son of mine.

LEARN MORE! READ THESE ARTICLES…
GWENDOLYN BROOKS • EMILY DICKINSON
WOLE SOYINKA

DID YOU KNOW?
Walker was left-handed, but her teachers in school forced her to write with her right hand. Not long ago, this practice was common in many places. Right-handedness was thought to be somehow 'better' and 'normal'.

Answer: Walker was the first Aboriginal woman to be published.

© Ed Kashi/Corbis

DID YOU KNOW?
After *Paula* was published, Allende suffered from severe writer's block. 'Writer's block' is the term used when a writer is unable to think what to write or how to write it. Allende eventually broke through by writing another non-fiction work.

The Letter Writer's Stories

Latin American writer Isabel Allende was born in 1942, in Lima, Peru. Her many books, written in Spanish, have been translated into several languages. Her works feature a **technique** called 'magic realism' - the use of fantasy and myth in realistic fiction. Her stories reflect her own experiences and also look at the role of women in Latin America.

Isabel Allende's uncle was Salvador Allende, president of Chile. She was a journalist there, as well as a short-story writer. In 1973, Salvador Allende was murdered during a time of political problems. Under the new government, Isabel Allende was threatened, and she and her husband and children were forced to flee to Venezuela. They ended up spending 13 years there.

In 1981, while still in **exile**, she started writing a letter to her dying grandfather. She wrote about childhood memories and the people who had touched their lives. This letter turned into her first novel, *La casa de los espíritus* (1982; *The House of the Spirits*). It was followed by the novels *De amor y de sombra* (1984; *Of Love and Shadows*), *Eva Luna* (1987), and *El plan infinito* (1991; *The Infinite Plan*).

Most of Allende's stories have a political **aspect** and include a number of exiles. Allende calls these people the '**marginals**'. She says that they are exiled from the big umbrella of society. They have the courage to stand on the edge of life and not be sheltered or protected.

In 1990, Allende was able to return to Chile. But she was heartbroken when her young daughter became sick and died of a terrible blood disease. Out of her sorrow came a book, *Paula* (1994). It was Allende's first **non-fiction** book and it went on to become a bestseller.

SEARCH LIGHT

Why do you suppose that Isabel Allende often writes about people who are exiles?

LEARN MORE! READ THESE ARTICLES...
JORGE LUIS BORGES • FRIDA KAHLO • JULES VERNE

Answer: Isabel Allende and her family became exiles themselves. It's not unusual for writers to draw on their own experiences for their work - even if it's fiction.

Writer of Life-Changing Stories

The famous English author Charles Dickens lived more than 100 years ago. Many of the stories he wrote were about how hard life could be for children. And many changes were made because of his books.

Some of Dickens' stories tell about how some children were treated badly in schools, at home, and at work. At his own school, his teacher beat

Charles Dickens.
© Bettmann/Corbis

him with a cane for laughing too loudly. Dickens was barely a teenager when he had to quit school and take a job away from home. His father had spent too much money and could not pay it back. He used many of his own experiences when he wrote his book *David Copperfield*.

When Dickens' stories were first read, some people were angry. Others were ashamed. Such stories as *Oliver Twist* made them think seriously. They realized that children should be treated kindly and should have fun as well as study hard. They should not be made to leave home and go to work when they are very young.

One of Dickens' best-known stories is called *A Christmas Carol*. It tells about a rich man called Scrooge who doesn't like Christmas. In fact, he doesn't like very much at all, except for making money. In the story, Scrooge learns that his life is better when he helps others and spends time enjoying their company.

People still like to read Dickens' books, not just to find out what life was like a long time ago but for the wonderful stories that they tell. Some are funny, like his *Pickwick Papers*. Some are family stories, such as *David Copperfield* and *Great Expectations*. And some of his books are historical stories, like *A Tale of Two Cities*.

LEARN MORE! READ THESE ARTICLES...
GWENDOLYN BROOKS • JULES VERNE • KATH WALKER

SEARCH LIGHT

True or false? Dickens' stories were entirely imaginary creations.

In this illustration from Dickens' *A Christmas Carol*, the miserly Ebenezer Scrooge is visited by the miserable ghost of his former partner, Jacob Marley.
© Bettmann/Corbis

 Answer: FALSE. Dickens used experiences from his own life and the lives of unfortunate children for some of his stories.

Journey to Everywhere

SEARCH LIGHT

How did studying geography and science help Verne's writing? (Hint: He liked to write about things that might happen.)

Imagine exploring a distant land in a giant balloon. You could drift over mountains and waterfalls, deep blue lakes, and flaming volcanoes.

Jules Verne.
© Rykoff Collection/Corbis

A French writer named Jules Verne imagined such a journey many years ago. He wrote about it in a book called *Five Weeks in a Balloon* (1863). It was his first adventure story about strange journeys. People liked the story so much that Verne decided to write more. The next one was called *A Journey to the Centre of the Earth* (1864). It was about all the wonderful and scary things people might find inside the Earth.

As a young boy Verne often went sailing with his brother on the River Loire in France. Verne would imagine that he was sailing a huge **yacht** on a voyage of discovery. Verne wrote about his imaginary adventures in the sea in *Twenty Thousand Leagues Under the Sea* (1870). He named his imaginary submarine the *Nautilus*, after an actual submarine built in 1800. In *From the Earth to the Moon* (1865) he wrote about travelling to the Moon in a rocketship long before powered flight was even possible.

People have said that Verne invented the future. It would be more accurate to say that he invented **science fiction**. Verne himself said that he was fortunate to live and write in a time when new discoveries and inventions were being made. He kept up with advances in geography and science to get ideas for his stories. Verne believed the discoveries he studied would someday make his imaginary journeys a reality.

LEARN MORE! READ THESE ARTICLES...
JORGE LUIS BORGES • CHARLES DICKENS • MARK TWAIN

Like many of Jules Verne's novels, *Twenty Thousand Leagues Under the Sea* is filled with fantastical creatures and exciting places.
© Bettmann/Corbis

DID YOU KNOW?
Not long after the success of Verne's book *Around the World in 80 Days* (1873), journalist Nellie Bly attempted the around-the-world journey. She finished in 72 days.

Answer: Studying geography helped Verne set his fantasy stories in realistic places to make them seem more real. His knowledge of science helped his invented machines seem more possible.

Rabindranath Tagore, seen here with his granddaughter in 1929, is generally considered the most outstanding artist of modern India.

SEARCH LIGHT

Rabindranath Tagore is famous as the first Indian to do what?

Poet Laureate
of India

Rabindranath Tagore, born in 1861 in Calcutta, India, started writing poems when he was only 8 years old. He grew up to be the first Indian writer to receive the Nobel Prize for Literature.

Tagore studied in India and London, England. In 1890 he published *Manasi*, his first collection of truly fine poems. In 1891 he went to East Bengal (now Bangladesh) to help manage his family's lands. He found the village people kind but very poor. Tagore wrote many poems and stories about their condition. He also wrote about the beautiful Bengali countryside, especially the Padma River.

Tagore wrote in new forms of verse and in the common language of the Bengali people, rather than in **classical** styles. His writings became very popular amongst all Bengalis. His poems of 1901-07 reflect his great sadness at the death of his wife and two of his children. In 1910 he wrote a little book of devotional songs called *Gitanjali*. It was translated into many languages and became a huge success. In 1913 he won the Nobel Prize for Literature.

Tagore produced 22 collections of writings during his life. He wrote songs, plays, short stories, and books, and he composed music. He also founded a school in rural West Bengal that combined European and Indian traditions. It later became Vishva-Bharati University.

In 1915 the British government knighted Tagore. Four years later he gave up his knighthood after a terrible shooting of Indians by British soldiers. All his life he spoke out against British rule of India.

Tagore lectured and read his works to people in many countries from about 1912. And at about age 70 he took up painting and became one of India's finest artists.

LEARN MORE! READ THESE ARTICLES…
BASHO • GWENDOLYN BROOKS • EMILY DICKINSON

DID YOU KNOW?

Rabindranath Tagore's father was a major Hindu thinker. He founded a quiet getaway in rural West Bengal (a state of India), where his son set up his experimental school.

Answer: Tagore is famous for being the first Indian to win the Nobel Prize for Literature.

31

Haiku Master

The poet Basho was born Matsuo Munefusa in 1644. He is considered to be the greatest of the Japanese *haiku* poets. Basho took his name from the Japanese term *basho-an*, meaning 'cottage of the plantain tree' (a plantain is like a banana). This was a simple place where the poet liked to go to be by himself.

Haiku is a traditional form of Japanese poetry that puts great emotion in just a few words. *Haiku* poems have only three lines and a total of only 17 syllables. And they are often about nature.

Although he was interested in poetry from a young age, Matsuo wasn't always a poet. He started out as a **samurai** warrior in the service of a local lord. But after his lord's death in 1666, Matsuo gave up being a warrior and focused on creating poetry. He moved to Japan's capital, Tokyo (at that time called Edo), and soon became well known as a poet and **critic**.

Basho brought a new style of *haiku* to Japanese poetry. In the past, it had basically been a hobby and not very serious, but Basho brought his Buddhist beliefs to his writing. He looked with interest at small things and showed the connections between all things. His new-style *haiku* compared two separate physical events. In the following *haiku*, for example, he links nightfall with the landing of a black crow.

On a withered branch
A crow has alighted:
Nightfall in autumn.

(Note: Unlike the original, this **translation** has only 16 syllables.)

Basho wrote poems as he traveled around the islands of Japan. He wrote about the sights and landscapes he saw, and these poems are considered some of his best.

LEARN MORE! READ THESE ARTICLES...
EMILY DICKINSON • AKIRA KUROSAWA • RABINDRANATH TAGORE

DID YOU KNOW?
A term often used to describe Basho's poetry is *sabi*. The word refers to a love of the old, the faded, and the little-noticed.

SEARCH LIGHT

Basho's name came from his
a) cottage.
b) village.
c) lord.

The Nobel Laureate

SEARCH LIGHT

Fill in the gap: Soyinka was imprisoned for disagreeing with the Nigerian _____.

When Wole Soyinka was a child, his grandfather told him how to deal with a bully. 'Even if you are beaten, challenge him again. I promise you, either you will defeat him or he will run away.'

These words turned out to be true for Wole Soyinka, the first black African writer to win the Nobel Prize for Literature. The bully he fought - with his words, not his fists - was the Nigerian military government. Even when the government put him into prison, he continued to write his stories, novels, essays, poetry, and plays.

Soyinka was born in 1934 in Nigeria. His full name is Akinwande Oluwole Soyinka. His large family is of Yoruba heritage. And having a big family, he got to listen to lots of stories - about battles, religion, legends, and family.

Soyinka attended university in England but returned to Nigeria to study African drama. He also taught drama and literature at Nigerian universities.

Wole Soyinka in 1986.
© Jacques Langevin/Corbis

In 1960 he founded a theatre group, where he put on his own plays and even acted in some. His first important play, *A Dance of the Forests*, was about Nigerian independence. In *The Lion and the Jewel*, Soyinka made fun of Westernized African school teachers.

During the Nigerian **civil war**, Soyinka worked for a cease-fire and was arrested because of his work and writings. The government placed him in a cell all by himself for over a year. Only his own ideas kept him entertained. These ideas became some of his later books.

Soyinka's plays draw on Nigerian culture, dance, poetry, music, and myths. These elements combine with his wide knowledge and his strong political beliefs to create powerful dramatic images and ideas.

LEARN MORE! READ THESE ARTICLES...
ISABEL ALLENDE • CHARLES DICKENS • KATH WALKER

Soyinka's plays have been staged worldwide. *Death and the King's Horseman* (shown here at the Goodman Theatre in Chicago, Illinois, U.S.) dramatizes the conflict between Western morals and African culture and traditions.
The Goodman Theatre; photo by James C. Clark

DID YOU KNOW?
Soyinka often refers to the Yoruba god Ogun as an important figure for him, his writing, and his people. He describes Ogun as 'the god of creativity and destruction'. Ogun is traditionally the god of war, the hunt, and ironworking.

Answer: Soyinka was imprisoned for disagreeing with the Nigerian government.

35

A Life of Letters and Literature

Emily Dickinson, one of America's greatest poets, was born in 1830 in Massachusetts, U.S. She had many friends, though she did not often leave her home to meet them. After 1865 she seldom left her room, appearing only occasionally and briefly in a white dress when guests visited downstairs.

Dickinson spent a great deal of time writing to her friends. The greatest excitement in Dickinson's life was in her **vivid** imagination. She included many of her best poems in the letters she wrote. She also wrote or copied poems into little booklets that she made by sewing pages together.

For the time in which she lived, Dickinson's poems were unusual. Most of them are about familiar things such as love and friendship, nature and death. But her rhymes are often not quite exact, and some of her poems are like a puzzle. But many people find great beauty and truth in her words.

Her poems are especially remarkable because of the strong effect they have, even though they're usually very brief. She stripped away unnecessary words and made sure that those that remained were **energetic** and exact. She also liked to place a familiar word in an unusual position to 'surprise' us and to make us pay attention.

Many people think that the poems of Emily Dickinson are among the best ever written by an American poet. It seems strange, then, that only seven of her poems were published while she was alive. It was Dickinson's sister, Lavinia, who first published her poems in a book. She called it *Poems by Emily Dickinson*. It was published in 1890, four years after Emily died.

LEARN MORE! READ THESE ARTICLES...
ISABEL ALLENDE • GWENDOLYN BROOKS
RABINDRANATH TAGORE

SEARCH LIGHT

Fill in the gap:
Dickinson often sent her poems in

_____

to her friends.

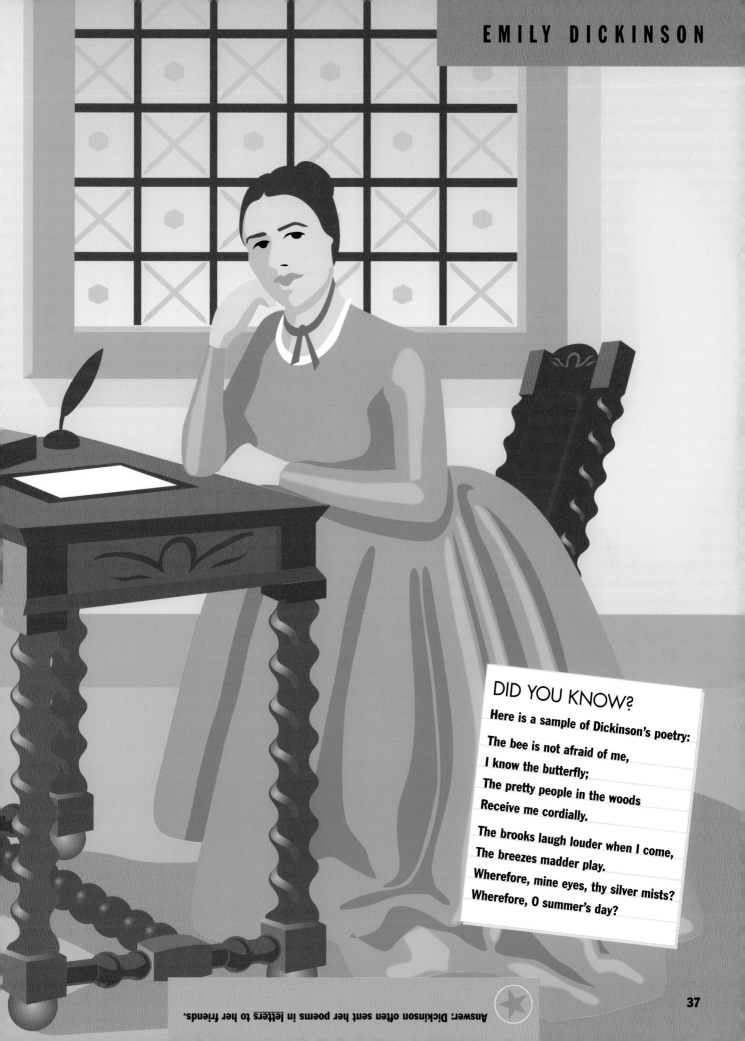

DID YOU KNOW?

Here is a sample of Dickinson's poetry:

The bee is not afraid of me,
I know the butterfly;
The pretty people in the woods
Receive me cordially.

The brooks laugh louder when I come,
The breezes madder play.
Wherefore, mine eyes, thy silver mists?
Wherefore, O summer's day?

Answer: Dickinson often sent her poems in letters to her friends.

37

Prized Poet
of Illinois

SEARCH LIGHT

Gwendolyn Brooks was the first African American poet to
a) win the Nobel Prize.
b) be published in the United States.
c) win the Pulitzer Prize.

Gwendolyn Brooks was born in 1917 and grew up in Chicago, Illinois, U.S. That city would play a major part in the life and work of this important American poet. She began writing poetry when she was just 7 years old. By the time she was in her early teens, her writing was being published in magazines.

Brooks, an African American, attended what was then the leading secondary school for white children in Chicago. This was very unusual at the time. She was later transferred to an all-black school and then to an **integrated** school. These experiences gave her an insight into the relationships between black people and white people that strongly influenced her work.

Gwendolyn Brooks with her first published book, *A Street in Bronzeville* (1945).
AP/Wide World Photos

Brooks's first published book, *A Street in Bronzeville* (1945), won rave reviews. Its poems made the ordinary life of her neighbours seem special to the reader. In 1950, Brooks won the Pulitzer Prize for Poetry with *Annie Allen*. She was the first African American poet to win this award. The book's poems focus on an African American girl growing up in Chicago.

In the late 1960s, Brooks's poetry became more **political**. She began to think that 'black poets should write as blacks, about blacks, and address themselves to blacks.' In 1968 she published *In the Mecca*. The book's long title poem reflects the pain and struggle of African American people living in the Mecca, a vast block of flats that had become part of a **slum**.

Brooks wrote many more books. She was honoured as **poet laureate** of Illinois (1968) and held a similar position for the whole United States (1985-86). Throughout her life Brooks remained strongly committed to teaching about the power of poetry and to encouraging young writers.

LEARN MORE! READ THESE ARTICLES...
ALVIN AILEY • EMILY DICKINSON • WOLE SOYINKA

DID YOU KNOW?

Gwendolyn Brooks, who helped so many young poets herself, was helped by others when she was young. The African American poets James Weldon Johnson and Langston Hughes personally urged her to read and write poetry.

Answer: c) win the Pulitzer Prize.

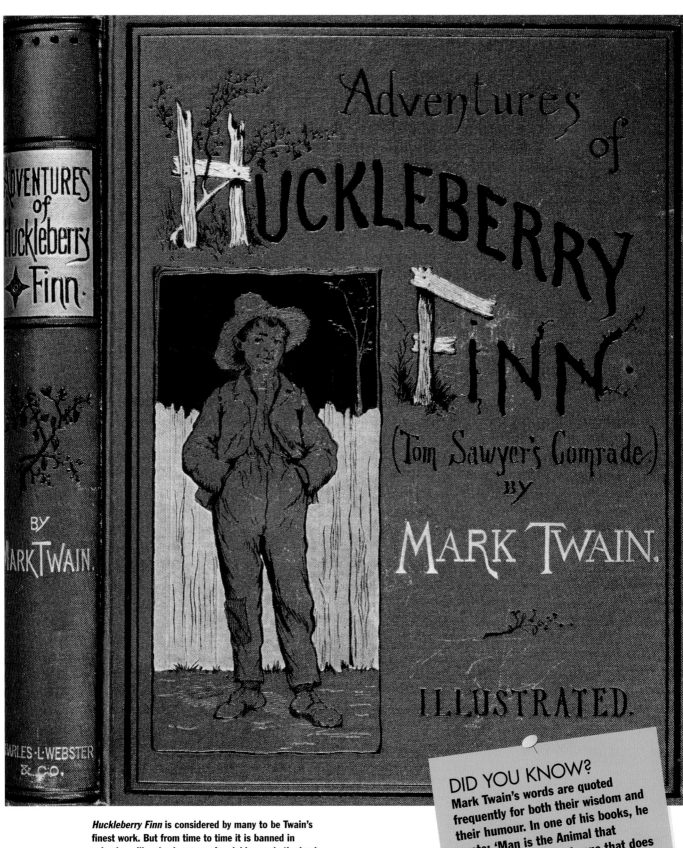

Huckleberry Finn is considered by many to be Twain's
finest work. But from time to time it is banned in
schools or libraries because of racial issues in the book.

© Stapleton Collection/Corbis

DID YOU KNOW?

Mark Twain's words are quoted
frequently for both their wisdom and
their humour. In one of his books, he
wrote: 'Man is the Animal that
Blushes. He is the only one that does
it - or has occasion to.' What do you
suppose he meant?

The Writer and the Mississippi River

A one time Mississippi River boat pilot, Mark Twain became one of America's greatest authors. His *Tom Sawyer*, *Huckleberry Finn*, and *Life on the Mississippi* rank high on any list of great American books.

Mark Twain was born Samuel Langhorne Clemens in 1835. He grew up in Hannibal, Missouri, on the Mississippi River. From this river town he gathered the material for his most famous stories. Young Tom Sawyer, for instance, was a combination of several boys - including himself.

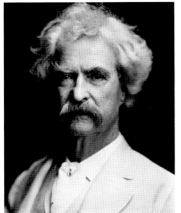

Mark Twain.
© Bettmann/Corbis

During his life, he held jobs that he would turn into material for his writing. His work as a riverboat pilot gave him experience he used to write *Life on the Mississippi*. When he began working as a newspaper reporter, he began using the pen-name Mark Twain. It is an old river term meaning two fathoms, or 12 feet, of water - a depth that was not very safe for riverboats.

One of his stories, 'The Celebrated Jumping Frog of Calaveras County', was printed in many newspapers. It was a popular story, and Twain travelled as a roving reporter and then on a lecture tour. After these travels he wrote *The Innocents Abroad*, which made him famous.

Twain was known as a humourist. But behind his mask of humour lay a serious view of life. He had known the sadness of poverty, the early death of his father and later his brother Henry, and the loss of a daughter. One of his most famous novels, *Huckleberry Finn*, is sometimes thought of as a child's book. But its heartbreak and wisdom are appreciated best by adults. Another of his famous novels, *Tom Sawyer*, is mostly a young person's book that adults can also read with pleasure.

SEARCH LIGHT

'Half twain' means 'mark twain plus half a mark' and equals 15 feet. So how much is a mark?

LEARN MORE! READ THESE ARTICLES...
LOUIS ARMSTRONG • CHARLES DICKENS • JULES VERNE

 Answer: A mark equals 6 feet. Mark twain, 12 feet, is two marks. Half twain is 2 1/2 marks, or 15 feet.

41

Theatrical Ballerina

Fanny Elssler was a famous Austrian dancer who brought energy and drama to her performances. She was born in 1810, in Vienna, Austria, and studied ballet from a young age. As a child, Elssler appeared with her sister in several ballets at Vienna's Kärntnerthor Theatre.

When she was a young adult, Elssler became famous worldwide thanks to her energetic spirit onstage and her remarkable pointe work (dancing on the points of the toes). She made her Paris Opéra debut in 1834 in Jean Coralli's ballet *La Tempête,* a dance version of William Shakespeare's play *The Tempest.*

Before Elssler came along, most ballet was 'classical ballet', which featured light graceful dance, like that performed by Elssler's greatest rival dancer, Marie Taglioni. But Elssler introduced theatrical, or 'character', ballet, which borrowed from folk dance traditions and even mime. She performed a Polish folk dance called the 'cracovienne' in the ballet *La Gypsy.* And because some Gypsies were associated with Spain, she got the nickname 'the Spaniard from the north'.

Elssler spent the later part of her career touring the United States, England, Germany, Italy, and Russia. Because of her long world tours, Elssler had to break her agreement with the Paris Opéra, and so she could not return to dance in France. Her worldwide tour ended up lasting more than ten years.

Elssler retired from the ballet in 1851. Her last years were spent in her native Vienna. During her career she was unequalled as a 'character' dancer with amazing dramatic powers.

LEARN MORE! READ THESE ARTICLES…
ALVIN AILEY • LUDWIG VAN BEETHOVEN • FRANCISCO DE GOYA

Fanny Elssler was known for her great dramatic skill. She was one of the first ballerinas to tour the United States. She was noted for her Spanish dances and often performed with her sister Therese.

Answer: Elssler's style of ballet borrowed from folk dance traditions.

DID YOU KNOW?
Bernhardt liked to keep her fans entertained and shocked, so she let it be known that she slept in a coffin every night. Though she slept mostly in an ordinary bed, she did pose for photographs 'asleep' in her coffin.

'The Divine Sarah'

GALWAY COUNTY LIBRARIES

Sarah Bernhardt, called 'the Divine Sarah' by playwright Oscar Wilde, was one of the greatest French actresses of the 19th century - and one of the most famous actresses of all time.

In 1861, at age 17, Bernhardt was enrolled in the acting course at the Paris Conservatoire. She admired some of her teachers. But she considered the school's methods too old-fashioned. Through a family

SEARCH LIGHT

Why do you think Sarah Bernhardt was nicknamed 'the Divine Sarah'?

Sarah Bernhardt in the title role of Victorien Sardou's play *Theodora*.
© Hulton-Deutsch Collection/Corbis

friend, Bernhardt was accepted into the national theatre company, the Comédie-Française. But she soon had to leave because she slapped a senior actress who had been rude to her younger sister. After a period when she questioned her talent for acting, Bernhardt joined the Odéon theatre and, in six years, established her reputation as an actress.

Building on her success, Bernhardt returned to the Comédie-Française. When she played the title role in Jean Racine's *Phédre*, she surprised the critics with the passion of her performance and was given excellent reviews. From that point on, she was a star. She performed in France and internationally. And she was in demand for new plays by major writers of the day, as well as for classics such as William Shakespeare's works. She even played a number of male roles, including Hamlet.

Bernhardt possessed a wide emotional range and could show sensitive detail in her acting. Her grace, striking looks, and charm gave her a **commanding** stage **presence**. And her unique voice was sometimes described as sounding like a 'golden bell'. Her popularity also increased because of her dramatic personality offstage.

In 1915 an earlier injury worsened and her right leg had to be removed. She continued to act, however, playing parts she could perform while seated.

LEARN MORE! READ THESE ARTICLES…
FANNY ELSSLER • WOLE SOYINKA • KIRI TE KANAWA

Poster of Sarah Bernhardt from the early 1900s.
© Historical Picture Archive/Corbis

Answer: Her wonderful acting, striking looks, and beautiful voice made Sarah Bernhardt seem to some like a goddess.

Living for Music

SEARCH LIGHT

Beethoven was Mozart's
a) teacher.
b) student.
c) father.

Can you imagine composing music without being able to hear it? Beethoven, one of the greatest music composers ever born, created much of his best music late in life, after he had become totally deaf.

Ludwig van Beethoven was born in 1770 in Bonn, Germany. Music was very important in his family. His grandfather and his father were professional singers in the choir of the **archbishop** in Bonn. Young Beethoven was given the opportunity to play the organ at court as soon as he was old enough to work. The archbishop liked his music so much that he sent him to Vienna to learn from Wolfgang Amadeus Mozart. After hearing Beethoven play, Mozart told his friends: 'This young man will make a great name for himself in the world.'

Beethoven's own handwritten music for his *Eroica* symphony.
Mansell/Timepix

At that time people usually thought of the piano as an instrument for playing music for singers. But Beethoven composed such beautiful piano music that it stood on its own as a work of art. Beethoven's music was a bridge between a strict musical tradition and a freer, more deeply emotional style of music. He also brought new ideas and life to such classical music forms as the sonata, symphony, concerto, and quartet. Some of his best-known works include the *Moonlight Sonata*, the *Pastoral* and *Eroica* symphonies, and the *Emperor Concerto*.

After some years Beethoven realized that he couldn't hear things clearly any more - not even what he was playing. Doctors told him he would never be cured. Beethoven stopped playing in public and kept away from people. But he still heard music in his mind and he wrote down his musical ideas in his notebooks. These books contained some of his finest music.

LEARN MORE! READ THESE ARTICLES...
LOUIS ARMSTRONG • FRANCISCO DE GOYA • RAVI SHANKAR

DID YOU KNOW?

Beethoven's musical works marked the beginnings of Romantic music. That sounds like music about love. But 'romantic' more broadly describes art that is concerned with expressing emotions, dramatic things in life, and the individual person's experience.

Answer: b) student.

Music at His Fingertips

SEARCH LIGHT

In 1930, at age 10, Ravi Shankar and other family members joined his eldest brother's Indian dance **troupe** in Paris, France. The boy lived in France for over five years and studied dance and music.

Shankar gave up dance at age 18. He returned to India and studied the sitar for seven years under master musician Ustad Allauddin Khan. The sitar is a large long-necked stringed instrument, played from a seated position.

In 1944 Shankar began composing film music. A bit later he became music director of All India Radio. His audience grew within India. And when his musical **score** for Satyajit Ray's 1955 film *Pather Panchali* won major awards, Shankar gained worldwide notice.

Shankar first toured the United States and England in 1956. Over the next ten years his audiences grew from small groups of Indian immigrants

Which instrument did Ravi Shankar play and make famous?
a) sitar
b) drums
c) cymbals

Ravi Shankar and daughter Anoushka performing at a charity concert in Kuala Lumpur, Malaysia, in 2001.
© AFP/Corbis

to sold-out concerts at New York City's Philharmonic Hall. As Shankar's fame increased, so did the popularity of Indian music. Sitar music is very different from music of the West. So it was exciting for Shankar and others to combine the two traditions to make altogether new sounds.

Shankar met and worked with many famous Western musicians who played a variety of styles. He played with jazz musicians, classical violinist Yehudi Menuhin, pianist and **conductor** André Previn, and experimental composer Philip Glass. His most famous musical association was with rock musician George Harrison of the Beatles. Harrison studied sitar under Shankar in India. Harrison's fame and influence allowed him to introduce Shankar and Indian music to a vast audience in the West.

Shankar continues to compose and perform. And he remains one of the most highly regarded musicians in the world.

LEARN MORE! READ THESE ARTICLES...
NUSRAT FATEH ALI KHAN • RABINDRANATH TAGORE • KIRI TE KANAWA

In 1971 George Harrison organized the Concert for Bangladesh.
Ravi Shankar and many other musicians performed to raise money
for the starving people of that country.
© Henry Diltz/Corbis

DID YOU KNOW?
The most frequently played South Asian musical form for sitar is called a *raga*. The sitarist, accompanied by *tabla* (drum) and *tamboura* (droning lute), plays a particular set of notes in a very specific way to create a unique mood.

A Vision in Motion

SEARCH LIGHT

Which of the following films is called *Seven Samurai* in English?
a) *Shichinin no samurai*
b) *Yoidore tenshi*
c) *Ikiru*

Film-maker Akira Kurosawa got his start working as an assistant director for a Japanese film studio. In 1943 he wrote and directed his first feature film, *Sanshiro Sugata*. The story of 19th-century **judo** masters became very popular with Japanese audiences.

Kurosawa's fame grew in 1948 with his film *Yoidore tenshi* (*Drunken Angel*). The film is about an alcoholic doctor who helps the poor fight against disease and **gangsters**. It stars Toshiro Mifune, who appeared in most of Kurosawa's films. In 1951 *Rashomon* made Kurosawa the first world-famous Japanese film-maker. The film won the Grand Prix at the Venice Film Festival and the Academy Award for best foreign film.

Many consider Kurosawa's best film to be *Ikiru* (*To Live*), from 1952. It follows a man who has only a few months to live and spends his last days helping the poor. Two

Kurosawa with American directors Francis Ford Coppola and George Lucas.
© The Kobal Collection—Toho/Kurosawa

Kurosawa's film *Ran* ('Chaos') is felt by many to be his finest work. It is a version of Shakespeare's play *King Lear* set in 16th-century Japan.
© The Kobal Collection/Herald Ace-Nippon—Herald-Greenwich

years later Kurosawa released his most popular film: *Shichinin no samurai* (*Seven Samurai*). The film is a **tribute** to American westerns - but with **samurai** warriors instead of cowboys. In fact, it was later remade in the United States as the western *The Magnificent Seven*.

Many of Kurosawa's films were set in historical Japan. But his work was popular in Japan and throughout the world. It combined artistic ideas, emotions, and images with plenty of action and drama to keep viewers entertained.

Kurosawa died in 1998. The Kurosawa Akira **Memorial** Satellite Studio has been opened on the Japanese island of Kyushu. It was there that he filmed several of his masterpieces, including *Ran* and *Kagemusha*.

LEARN MORE! READ THESE ARTICLES...
BASHO • SARAH BERNHARDT • WOLE SOYINKA

Answer: a) *Shichinin no samurai*

New Zealand's Opera Star

Kiri Te Kanawa was born in 1944 in New Zealand. At the age of 5 weeks, she was adopted. Her adoptive and biological mothers were both of British descent. Her adoptive and biological fathers were Maori (native New Zealanders).

Te Kanawa's mother discovered very early that her daughter was musical. So her parents sent her to a school where a well-known singer taught music. After leaving school Te Kanawa won various singing competitions in New Zealand and Australia.

By the 1970s Te Kanawa was world famous as a **soprano** diva (leading female vocalist) of opera. Her first big success was in Wolfgang Amadeus Mozart's opera *The Marriage of Figaro*. She performed in many Mozart operas after that.

Te Kanawa made her first appearance at the Metropolitan Opera in New York City quite by accident. The lead star playing Desdemona in Giuseppe Verdi's *Otello* suddenly fell ill. Te Kanawa was asked to perform instead, with only three hours to rehearse! She did such a splendid job that everyone raved about her performance.

In 1981 Te Kanawa sang at the wedding of Britain's Prince Charles and Princess Diana. She sang George Frideric Handel's 'Let the Bright

Te Kanawa filming a video.
© Le Poer Trench Michael—Sygma/Corbis

Seraphim'. This performance was seen on television by millions of viewers all over the world.

Te Kanawa is particularly known for the warmth of her soprano voice and her engaging personality on the stage. She has made a number of recordings. Most of these are of classical pieces, but she has also recorded traditional Maori songs from her New Zealand childhood.

In 1982 Te Kanawa was given a British noble title. She was made Dame Kiri Te Kanawa for the joy her singing had brought to so many.

LEARN MORE! READ THESE ARTICLES...
LUDWIG VAN BEETHOVEN • NUSRAT FATEH ALI KAHN • KATH WALKER

Dame Kiri Te Kanawa appears here in Richard Strauss's comedic opera *Arabella*.
© Robbie Jack/Corbis

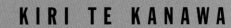

DID YOU KNOW?

In 1990, during a tour of Australia and New Zealand, Kiri Te Kanawa performed at an outdoor concert in the city of Auckland. An audience of 140,000 people attended.

Answer: FALSE. She is a soprano.

Here, Nusrat Fateh Ali Khan and Party perform in a 1993 concert. The term 'party' is a general term for the group of musicians who play for the *qawwal*.

© BALDEV/Corbis Sygma

Centre Stage of *Qawwali*

Nusrat Fateh Ali Khan was considered one of the greatest singers of the music known as *qawwali*. Begun in Persia (present-day Iran) hundreds of years ago, *qawwali* music is based on Sufi Muslim poems about deep religious faith expressed through love. It has simple melodies and forceful rhythms.

*Qawwal*s (singers of *qawwali*) traditionally perform their songs at **shrines**. A *qawwal* must learn all the Sufi poems. He often makes up more

Nusrat Fateh Ali Khan in concert.
Michael Harder Photography

*qawwali*s by using phrases and passages from different poems to create a new expression or idea. The singing includes much shouting and dancing.

Nusrat Fateh Ali Khan was born in 1948 in Pakistan. His father and two of his uncles were also famous *qawwal*s who sang in the classical style. Khan received music lessons from his father. When his father died in 1964, Khan sang in the *qawwali* style for the first time at his father's funeral. Two years later Khan gave his first public performance, singing with his uncles.

Khan sang in a very high range (a family trademark) and had a powerfully expressive voice. He was noted for his melodic creativity and had been known to perform for 10 hours. By the early 1970s Khan was recognized throughout Pakistan as the outstanding *qawwal* of his time. He sang at a world music concert in the United Kingdom in 1985. Soon he was performing regularly throughout Europe.

In 1996 Khan recorded songs for several American films. He also appeared on music television shows and performed songs that appealed specifically to Western audiences. Some people felt that he had betrayed the music's Islamic heritage. But Khan said he had given up nothing to share his musical heritage with a wider audience.

LEARN MORE! READ THESE ARTICLES...
HASSAN FATHY • RAVI SHANKAR • KIRI TE KANAWA

SEARCH LIGHT

Fill in the gaps: *Qawwali* music is based on _____ _____.

Answer: *Qawwali* music is based on Sufi poetry.

Enriching American Dance

Alvin Ailey was born in 1931, in Texas, U.S. As a child, he helped his mother pick cotton to earn money. They moved to Los Angeles when Ailey was about 11 years old.

In Los Angeles, Ailey discovered dance during a school field trip to a ballet performance. He began to study with the dance

Alvin Ailey in 1983.
© Bettmann/Corbis

teacher Lester Horton and joined the Lester Horton Dance Theater in 1949. When Horton died four years later Ailey became the director of the company. However, the next year the company broke up and Ailey moved to New York City.

In New York Ailey danced in many performances and worked with some famous dance **choreographers**. They included Martha Graham and Hanya Holm. Ailey's own modern dancing combined what he learned from Lester Horton with African and Afro-Caribbean styles.

SEARCH LIGHT

Ailey began his professional dancing in
a) the 1950s.
b) the 1940s.
c) the 1980s.

In 1958 Ailey formed the Alvin Ailey American Dance Theater. Most of its members were African Americans, like Ailey. One of the company's early performances was a work by Ailey called *Revelations*. The dance is set to American **Negro spirituals**, and it has become the company's most popular work.

Since the 1960s Ailey's company has performed around the United States and the world. Its popularity made Ailey one of the most famous American choreographers in the world and encouraged people everywhere to appreciate and enjoy modern dance.

Alvin Ailey died in 1989, but the Alvin Ailey American Dance Theater continues to **flourish**. And just as Ailey hoped, the company he founded has expanded from a troupe of mostly black performers to a rich multi-ethnic mix.

LEARN MORE! READ THESE ARTICLES...
LOUIS ARMSTRONG • GWENDOLYN BROOKS • FANNY ELSSLER

Alvin Ailey's dance *Revelations* is the company's signature piece. Since it is set to the religious music of his childhood, the name is quite appropriate. Revelation is the name of the last book of the Christian New Testament.

© Hulton-Deutsch Collection/Corbis

DID YOU KNOW?

Ailey choreographed 79 ballets during his lifetime. Altogether, however, the Alvin Ailey American Dance Theater has performed over 170 works created by more than 65 choreographers.

Louis Armstrong (centre) also performed in a number of films. This picture is from *High Society*, a 1956 film starring the singer Bing Crosby (seated, far left), Frank Sinatra, and Grace Kelly.
The Kobal Collection/MGM

SEARCH LIGHT

What is unusual about scat? (Hint: Bee dee wa scabba doo.)

Satchmo – Jazz Superstar

In the early 20th century, a young African American boy sang and danced on a street in New Orleans, Louisiana. He wanted to earn some money because his family was very poor. That boy, Louis Daniel Armstrong, would become one of the world's most famous jazz trumpet players.

Armstrong loved music and tried various instruments before finally choosing the cornet. The cornet looks like a trumpet but is shaped like a cone. Armstrong became the leader of his school band. Jazz was just becoming popular, and as a teenager he learned music by listening to pieces played by famous jazz musicians. Later he learned to read music.

Armstrong warming up on his trumpet in 1956.
© Ted Streshinsky/Corbis

Armstrong played with jazz bands in Chicago and New York City. He recorded his first solo pieces, 'Chimes Blues' and 'Tears', in Chicago. In New York he changed from the cornet to the trumpet. He thought the trumpet had a brighter sound and a more flamboyant look. By the time Armstrong was 28 years old he had become very famous. He toured the world as a trumpet soloist with big bands.

Louis Armstrong was nicknamed 'Satchmo' by his fellow musicians. Short for 'Satchel Mouth', the name suggested that his mouth was as wide as a satchel (a large school bag). But the friendly teasing was a sign of the great respect jazz musicians had for Armstrong's talent. His creativity, ability to express emotion, and superior **technical** skill were universally admired.

Armstrong is also remembered as one of the inventors of what is called 'scat'. Sometimes, while singing a **lyric**, he would sing without using words. He would sing a string of sounds instead. His scat singing and gravelly voice became as well known as his face and trumpet.

LEARN MORE! READ THESE ARTICLES…
ALVIN AILEY • LUDWIG VAN BEETHOVEN • RAVI SHANKAR

Answer: Scat is singing that uses sounds rather than real words.

DID YOU KNOW?
Kermit the Frog's original eyes were made from a Ping-Pong ball cut in half.

Muppet Master

As a puppeteer and creator of the Muppets, Jim Henson delighted, entertained, and educated several generations of children and adults.

Henson was born in Mississippi, U.S., in 1936. He grew up in Washington, D.C., and began his career as a puppeteer while in secondary school there. Later he and his wife had a short puppet show on local television called 'Sam and Friends'. While he was still in university, Henson put together a team of puppeteers who performed in commercials and on TV.

Jim Henson's granddaughters Katrina (left) and Virginia Henson with Kermit the Frog when he was given his own star on the Hollywood Walk of Fame in 2002.
© Reuters Newmedia Inc./Corbis

In 1969 the Children's Television Workshop created a TV show with Henson called 'Sesame Street'. The program featured his 'Muppets' and included such now well-known characters as Kermit the Frog, Grover, Big Bird, and Cookie Monster. Young viewers loved the Muppets. But 'Sesame Street' also proved Henson's belief that learning could be fun.

The Muppets are a unique form of puppetry that was new to television. Often it takes two people to operate a Muppet since the head and each arm may require a human hand to move them. The larger Muppets, like Snuffleupagus and Big Bird, are actually costumed actors. The puppeteer who controls each Muppet also provides the character's voice. Henson operated and voiced Kermit himself for 35 years.

'Sesame Street' was so successful that in 1976 Henson created 'The Muppet Show' - a TV programme for both adults and children. The Muppets have appeared in several films as well, including *The Muppet Movie* and *Muppets from Space*.

Sadly, Henson died suddenly of pneumonia in 1990. But his Muppets continue to perform today, with Henson's son Brian leading the company.

SEARCH LIGHT

Henson's first TV show was called
a) 'Cheers'.
b) 'Sam and Friends'.
c) 'The Banana Bunch'.

LEARN MORE! READ THESE ARTICLES...
CHARLES DICKENS • WOLE SOYINKA • MARK TWAIN

Jim Henson, seen here among some of his Muppets, was a favourite with both children and adults. Some adults enjoyed Henson's work from the time they were children themselves.

Answer: b) 'Sam and Friends'.

affordable reasonable in price

archaeology (adjective: archaeological) the science that deals with past human life as shown by fossils, tools, and other material left by ancient peoples

archbishop high-ranking priest in some Christian churches who oversees other bishops and church government in a very large area

aspect part, feature, or quality of something

choreographer creator of a dance

civil war war between opposing groups of citizens of the same country

classical traditional in style

commanding grand and powerful

commission (verb) to order to be made; (noun) an order granting the power to perform various acts or duties

compose to create a literary, musical, or other artistic work

conductor the leader of an orchestra

critic person who studies and comments on the quality of performances or works of art

depict to represent by a picture

dictate to speak for another person to write down or for a machine to record

energetic lively or active

exile banishment or official separation

fantastical highly imaginative and unrealistic

flourish to grow successfully; to do well

fresco painting done on freshly spread moist plaster

gangster member of a gang of criminals

gory violent and bloody

humanitarian devoted to the happiness and welfare of other people

inspiration something that causes a particular thought, feeling, or idea

integrate (adjective: integrated) to combine two or more parts in order to create a more balanced whole; *especially*, to remove barriers that isolate one group of people from another

judo sport, developed from the Japanese fighting art of *jujitsu*, in which opponents use quick movements and careful positioning to try to throw each other to the ground

landscape picture showing views of nature and the countryside

lyrics the words of a song

marginal lying at or near the outer edge (margin) of some larger place, object, or group

memorial something that keeps alive the memory of a person or event

mural a painting on a wall

Negro spiritual religious folk song developed among blacks in the southern United States

non-fiction literature that is based on fact rather than on imagination

poet laureate poet honoured by a country or other region as its most outstanding poet

political having to do with creating and controlling a government

presence the strong and self-confident quality a person has that makes others focus on him or her

samurai warrior class in Japan from about the 12th to the mid-19th century

science fiction stories that deal with the effects of real or imagined science on society or individuals

score in films, the background music that goes with the pictures on the screen

self-portrait picture of the artist who painted or drew the picture; usually shows the face

seraphim in Christianity, Islam, and Judaism, special angels who guard God's throne

shrine place where honour or worship is offered to a saint or deity

slum crowded, dirty, run-down housing

soprano the highest woman's singing voice; also, a person who sings in this voice

tapestry heavy cloth that has designs or pictures woven into it and that is often used as a wall hanging

technical having to do with the way a skilled individual handles the details of an art or craft

technique special way of doing something; *especially*, the way a skilled individual handles the details of an art or craft

translation version of a written work that has been changed from its original language into another

tribute gift, performance, or action meant to show appreciation, respect, or caring for someone or something

troupe company or group; *especially*, a working group of stage performers

vivid bright or dramatic

yacht small ship or large boat used for pleasure cruising or racing

I N D E X